Secrets
of the
Space
Shuttle

© 2008 Weldon Owen Education Inc. All rights reserved.

Library of Congress Cataloging-in-Publication Data

Rees, Peter.
  Secrets of the space shuttle / By Peter Rees.
     p. cm. -- (Shockwave)
  Includes index.
  ISBN-10: 0-531-17590-1 (lib. bdg.)
  ISBN-13: 978-0-531-17590-3 (lib. bdg.)
  ISBN-10: 0-531-18818-3 (pbk.)
  ISBN-13: 978-0-531-18818-7 (pbk.)
  1. Space shuttles--Juvenile literature. I. Title. II. Series.

  TL795.515.R44 2007
  629.44′1--dc22

2007016731

Published in 2008 by Children's Press, an imprint of Scholastic Inc.,
557 Broadway, New York, New York 10012
www.scholastic.com

08 09 10 11 12 13 14 15 16 17
10 9 8 7 6 5 4 3 2 1

Printed in China through Colorcraft Ltd., Hong Kong

Author: Peter Rees
Educational Consultant: Ian Morrison
Editor: Nerida Frost
Designer: Carol Hsu
Photo Researchers: Jamshed Mistry and Nadja Embacher

Photographs by: Getty Images (space tourist, p. 27); **Jennifer and Brian Lupton** (teenagers,
pp. 32–33); **NASA/National Aeronautics and Space Administration: Human Spaceflight**
(p. 26); astronauts, drinking, with shampoo, pp. 18–19; pp. 20–21; orange-suited astronaut,
p. 22; astronaut training programme, p. 24; pool practice, emergency evacuation, pp. 24–25;
Hubble telescope, p. 28; settlement on the moon, p. 30; colony on the moon, pp. 32–33;
GRIN: Great Images in NASA (pp. 3–9; Robert Goddard, p. 11; rocket and crane, Yuri Gagarin,
pp. 12–13; moon, *Apollo 11* astronauts, pp. 14–17; astronaut exercising, pp. 18–19; suspended
astronaut, pp. 22–23; zero gravity, pp. 24–25; International Space Station modules, pp. 26–27;
p. 31); **Photolibrary** (USSR rocket, pp. 10–11); Spacescapes (supernova, pp. 28–29); **Tranz/Corbis**
(Laika, p. 13; dish antenna, p. 29)

All illustrations and other photographs © Weldon Owen Education Inc.

Secrets
of the
Space
Shuttle

Peter Rees

children's press®

An imprint of Scholastic Inc.

NEW YORK • TORONTO • LONDON • AUCKLAND • SYDNEY
MEXICO CITY • NEW DELHI • HONG KONG
DANBURY, CONNECTICUT

CHECK THESE OUT!

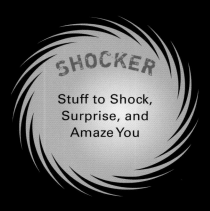

SHOCKER

Stuff to Shock,
Surprise, and
Amaze You

Quick Recaps
and Notable
Notes

Word Stunners
and Other Oddities

The Heads-Up
on Expert Reading

Links to More
Information

CONTENTS

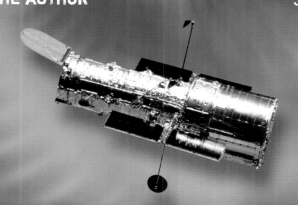

astronaut (*ASS truh nawt*) someone who travels in space

booster a rocket engine used as the main source of thrust in the takeoff of a rocket or missile

cosmonaut (*KOZ muh nawt*) an astronaut from Russia or the former USSR

gravity the force that pulls objects toward each other; the larger the object, the more gravity it exerts

Mission Control the command center for monitoring, steering, and supporting U.S. spacecraft

zero gravity weightlessness experienced outside a planet's gravity. Zero gravity is also called microgravity, because even in space there is always a tiny amount of gravity present.

. . . .

For additional vocabulary, see Glossary on page 34.

The word *astronaut* comes from the Greek *astron*, meaning "star" and *nautes*, meaning "sailor." So astronaut actually means "star sailor."

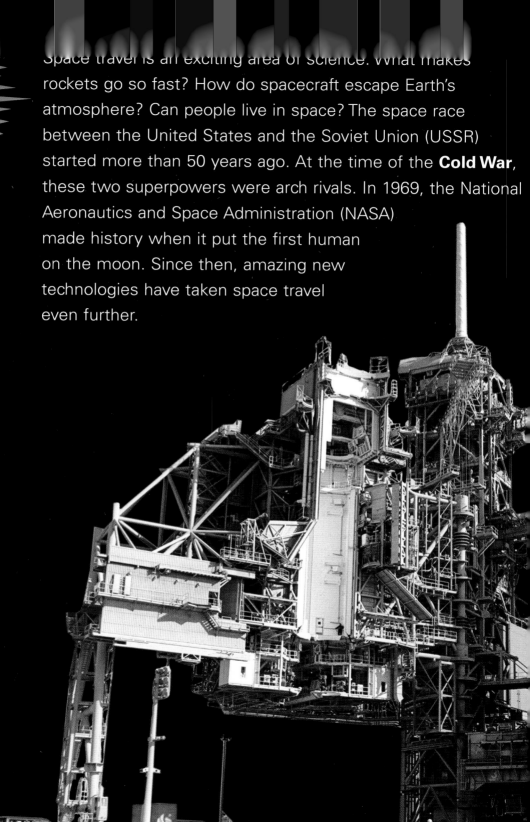

Space travel is an exciting area of science. What makes rockets go so fast? How do spacecraft escape Earth's atmosphere? Can people live in space? The space race between the United States and the Soviet Union (USSR) started more than 50 years ago. At the time of the **Cold War**, these two superpowers were arch rivals. In 1969, the National Aeronautics and Space Administration (NASA) made history when it put the first human on the moon. Since then, amazing new technologies have taken space travel even further.

Today, space shuttles carry space crews, **satellites**, and other equipment into space. One of the newest space projects, the International Space Station (ISS), is putting teams of **astronauts** from around the world into space for research. For the space explorers of the twenty-first century, the sky is certainly *not* the limit!

Space shuttle *Discovery* on the launchpad

Milestones in Space Exploration

1957 First artificial satellite – *Sputnik* (USSR)

1957 First living thing in space – a dog named Laika (USSR)

1961 First person in space – Yuri Gagarin (USSR)

1962 First American to orbit Earth – John Glenn (USA)

1963 First woman in space – Valentina Tereshkova (USSR)

1965 First space walk – Aleksei Leonov (USSR)

1969 First people on the moon – Neil Armstrong and Buzz Aldrin (USA)

1971 First manned space station – *Salyut 1* (USSR)

1973 First U.S. space station – *Skylab*

1981 First space shuttle – *Columbia* (USA)

1983 First American woman in space – Sally Ride

1990 Hubble Space Telescope (USA)

1998 First modules of the ISS

2004 First spacecraft orbits Saturn (USA)

2006 *New Horizons* launched to fly by Pluto in 2015 (USA)

Space Quest

In the twentieth century, space became the new frontier of science and of human endurance. After centuries of observing the stars through telescopes, people were no longer content simply to gaze at the sky. They wanted to explore it. In 1903, the Wright brothers completed the first successful power-driven airplane flight. Everything seemed possible. The dream of flying into space became feasible.

In the 1920s, early rocket science pioneers, such as the Soviet Konstantin Tsiolkovsky and the American Robert Goddard, laid the foundations for later space explorations. Their experiments encouraged a whole generation of scientists from around the world to pursue the dream of exploring space.

In the 1930s, rocketry really took off. In Germany, the USSR, and the United States, scientists were making great strides. In 1944, the Jet Propulsion Laboratory (JPL) was founded at the California Institute of Technology. In 1958, NASA was formed to take over the space program. Its job was to put the United States at the forefront of the space race.

NASA and USSR are both short forms. NASA is an acronym, because it is pronounced as a word. USSR, on the other hand, is an abbreviation. Each letter is pronounced separately.

Rocket Men

Konstantin Tsiolkovsky (1857–1935) was the father of Soviet rocketry. In 1923, he published a book that many consider the first academic work on rocketry. He invented the multistage rocket. However, he never built a rocket himself.

In 1933, Sergei Korolev and his research group launched the USSR's first liquid-fuel rocket. Korolev later designed the spacecraft that carried the first **cosmonaut** into space.

Solid-fuel Rockets

Fuel

Liquid-fuel Rockets

Fuel tank

Oxidant

Combustion chamber

Pumps

Nozzle

Solid-fuel rockets are packed with fuel that burns around a hollow center. These rockets cannot be turned off once they have been **ignited**.

Liquid-fuel rockets can be twice as powerful as solid-fuel rockets. They are also more controllable, because they can be turned on and off to create more or less **thrust**.

Tsiolkovsky is recognized for his contributions to rocketry on this **commemorative** stamp from the USSR.

Robert Goddard (1882–1945) invented the liquid-fuel rocket in 1926. During his lifetime, his vision of rocket-powered spaceflight was treated as science fiction by many. Today, he is also recognized as one of the fathers of modern rocketry.

The Space Race

The United States and the Soviet Union set out to beat each other in the "space race." Both countries invested staggering sums in building ever-larger rockets. Rockets are the only things powerful enough to propel a spacecraft into orbit. However, early rockets were unpredictable. Sometimes they rose only a few feet before crashing back to the ground in flames. Sometimes they spiraled wildly out of control.

Some early rockets launched animals into space. The first attempts to put people into space were very dangerous. Astronauts were stuffed into tiny capsules on top of towering rockets. There was still very little known about the effects of space travel on health.

On April 12, 1961, a Soviet cosmonaut named Yuri Gagarin was blasted into space from a top-secret site in Kazakhstan. His orbit around Earth in the tiny *Vostok* capsule lasted less than two hours, but it shook the world. The United States suddenly realized that it had fallen behind in the space race. Just a few weeks after Gagarin's historic flight, the U.S. launched astronaut Alan Shepard into space on May 5, 1961.

This rocket launched Alan Shepard into space. Although Shepard didn't go into orbit as Yuri Gagarin had done, he was the first man to return to Earth with his spaceship. Gagarin parachuted from his spaceship before landing.

After his spaceflight, Yuri Gagarin became a hero in the USSR and a worldwide celebrity. He traveled widely, **promoting** the achievements of his country.

What Do You Think?

Laika, the Soviet space dog, went from being a stray on the streets of Moscow to being an international celebrity after becoming the first animal to orbit Earth on November 3, 1957. Sadly, Laika was not able to enjoy her fame. She died during her flight. Laika was not the only animal to die in space. Do you think it was worth sacrificing animals to make rockets safer for people?

Mission: Moon

Earth's bright satellite, the moon, has been worshipped, sung to, and even blamed for bringing out werewolves and other monsters. In the seventeenth century, astronomers first aimed telescopes at the moon and saw what they thought were dark oceans. Some imagined creatures living there. By the twentieth century, the moon was known to be a dusty, dead world. What had looked like dark oceans turned out to be vast **lava** plains. Yet much was still unknown about our nearest neighbor. It was only natural that scientists would want to go there.

The origin of the moon lies in an astonishing event that occurred about four billion years ago. An object the size of Mars appeared from space and slammed into Earth. A cloud of rubble flew into orbit and clumped together to form the moon.

On July 20, 1969, Commander Neil Armstrong of *Apollo 11* stepped onto the moon. It was the crowning achievement of the space race. The Soviets had beaten the United States to the moon with unmanned space probes. However, the United States had been determined not to be left behind by its rival. It put the first person on the moon, securing the American space program its place in history.

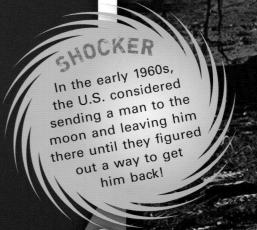

SHOCKER

In the early 1960s, the U.S. considered sending a man to the moon and leaving him there until they figured out a way to get him back!

Neil Armstrong's first steps on the moon were watched by millions on TV. As Armstrong stepped onto the moon's surface, he said, "That's one small step for man, one giant leap for mankind."

Armstrong's words became famous. However, his quote was a mistake! He meant to say "... one small step for *a* man, ..." Even Armstrong himself doesn't know if he botched his lines in the excitement or if static in the radio transmission blotted out the "a."

Early astronauts were treated like superheroes when they returned to Earth. New York City welcomed the three *Apollo 11* astronauts, Neil Armstrong, Michael Collins, and Buzz Aldrin, in the largest parade the city had ever had.

Secrets of the Space Shuttle

The huge Saturn rockets that carried astronauts to the moon were impressive, but they were also wasteful. Each expensive rocket could be used only once before plunging into the ocean. Scientists began dreaming of a reusable spacecraft. It would carry satellites, cargo, and experiments into orbit and land again safely like an airplane. On April 12, 1981, they got their wish with the launch of the first space shuttle, *Columbia*. Apart from the fuel tank, nearly every part of *Columbia* was recyclable. The rocket **boosters** were even retrieved from the ocean and reused.

Space shuttles look like ordinary airplanes. However, with three rocket engines, jets in the nose for steering, and the ability to survive 2,500 degree temperatures, a shuttle is far from ordinary! Altogether, five fully operational space shuttles have been built. Tragically, two shuttles, *Challenger* and *Columbia*, were destroyed in accidents that shocked the world.

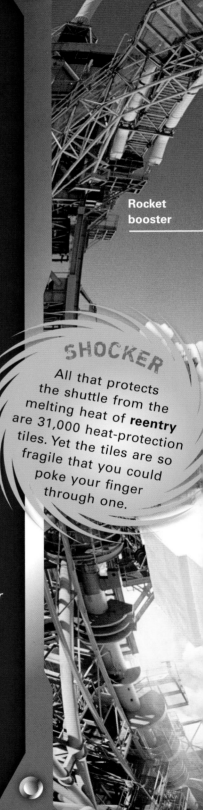

Rocket booster

SHOCKER

All that protects the shuttle from the melting heat of **reentry** are 31,000 heat-protection tiles. Yet the tiles are so fragile that you could poke your finger through one.

Space Shuttle Facts
- a reusable spacecraft
- 3 rocket engines
- jets in the nose for steering
- solid-fuel boosters
- 31,000 heat-protection tiles

Space shuttles are powered into orbit by their own liquid-fuel rockets, as well as two solid-fuel rocket boosters. The boosters and huge fuel tank are **jettisoned** when they are used up.

Fuel tank

Three, Two, One ... Liftoff!

When conditions are safe for liftoff, the last few seconds are counted down. As the rocket streaks upward, acceleration forces the astronauts down into their seats.

Above the World

The burnt-out rocket detaches and falls back to Earth. The space shuttle is left in orbit, 100 to 300 miles above Earth. Even from this height, astronauts can still see structures such as cities and airports.

Feeling the Heat

Reentry into Earth's atmosphere is one of the most dangerous parts of the flight. **Friction** with the air results in tremendous heat on the spacecraft.

Touchdown

Shuttles land by gliding down to Earth. The pilot makes a series of steep turns to slow down. Parachutes pop out the back to help bring the shuttle to a stop.

Losing Weight

Many people think that a space shuttle in orbit is "floating" in space. In fact, orbiting spacecraft are not floating, they are falling! Imagine throwing a ball so hard that it zoomed over the horizon. The ball would go so fast that, although **gravity** would pull it down, it would fall in a curve that is the same as the curve of Earth. Therefore, it would never get any closer to the ground.

The speed needed to do this is 17,300 miles per hour. That is the speed at which the space shuttle normally travels in orbit. Moving at this speed keeps the shuttle falling around the Earth without actually touching it. If it were to slow down or stop, it would drop back to Earth like a stone. Everyone aboard is falling too. That is why they feel weightless – just as you do when you bounce high on a trampoline.

Most astronauts say being weightless is fun. However, it takes some getting used to.

Daily Life in Space

It's impossible to shower while in orbit. So astronauts keep clean with washcloths and rinseless soap. They even wash their hair this way.

Liquids form into balls in space, so astronauts drink through straws from sealed containers. They usually eat precooked meals that are sealed in containers as well. There are also plenty of snacks on board.

SHOCKER

Normal toilets don't work in space. The toilets on a space shuttle work by suction. Before going into space, astronauts have to train on a special toilet-training device!

Living in weightlessness can have serious effects on an astronaut's health. Bones lose mass and become brittle. Muscles begin to waste away. Astronauts lose red blood cells, making them easily tired. Astronauts are sometimes so weakened after a long spaceflight that they need to be helped from their spacecraft. Exercising for one to two hours a day while in space can help counter these effects.

Did You Know?

Using tools in space can be difficult. In weightlessness, a twist of a wrench will set the astronaut spinning instead of the nut! Astronauts must keep their feet firmly attached to the shuttle.

Working and Walking in Space

Two astronauts on each mission are trained and outfitted for Extravehicular Activity (EVA), or spacewalking. Other crew members do science experiments and make repairs. If they have time, they do exercise to maintain physical fitness.

For EVA, the astronauts put on their space suits and leave the shuttle through an airlock that prevents the shuttle's air from leaking into space. A typical space walk might involve removing a satellite from the shuttle's **payload bay** and placing it in orbit. A robotic arm is used, although in space, even a satellite weighing several tons can be moved easily by hand.

During EVA, astronauts are tied to the space shuttle. Even if they come unattached, they wouldn't be left behind, since they are moving at the same speed as the shuttle – about 17,300 miles per hour.

> Sometimes when things don't make complete sense, reading on can help. "Space walk" didn't make sense to me until I read on and discovered it just meant work outside the spacecraft.

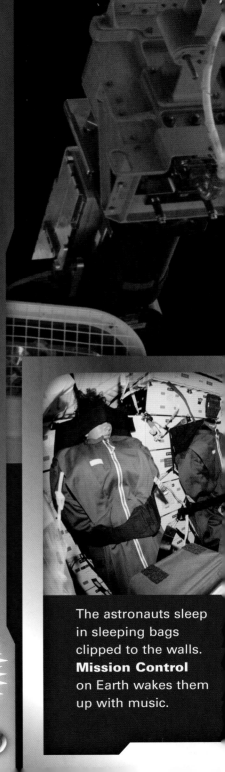

The astronauts sleep in sleeping bags clipped to the walls. **Mission Control** on Earth wakes them up with music.

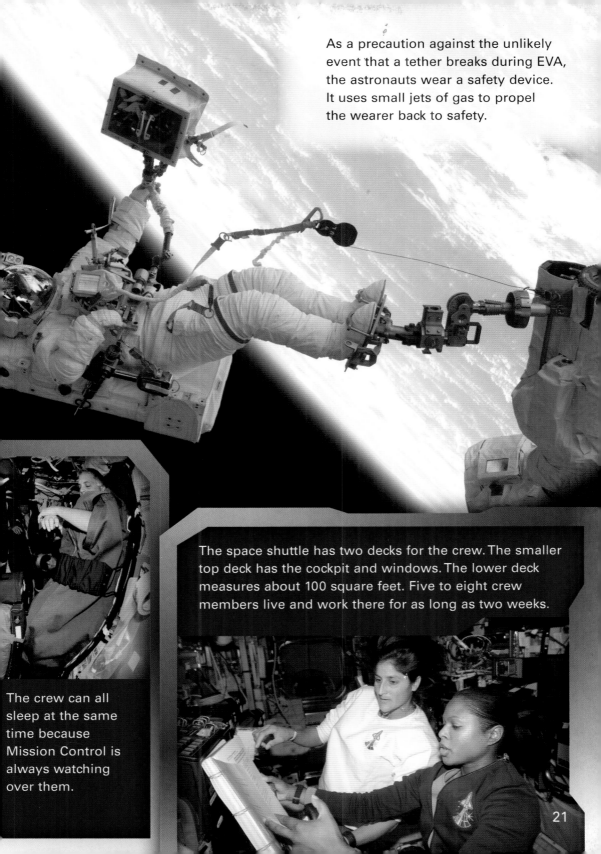

As a precaution against the unlikely event that a tether breaks during EVA, the astronauts wear a safety device. It uses small jets of gas to propel the wearer back to safety.

The space shuttle has two decks for the crew. The smaller top deck has the cockpit and windows. The lower deck measures about 100 square feet. Five to eight crew members live and work there for as long as two weeks.

The crew can all sleep at the same time because Mission Control is always watching over them.

Inside the Suit

The vacuum of space is one of the most hostile environments humans have ever visited. Outside of Earth's protective atmosphere, sunlight fries objects with a scorching heat, and shade brings freezing cold. EVA astronauts are bombarded with deadly radiation, while even a tiny **meteoroid** could kill.

Without a tough, specially designed space suit, the astronauts would become rapidly **unconscious**. Their blood and bodily fluids would boil in the low pressure. Within minutes, they would die. An EVA space suit can keep an astronaut alive in space for about nine hours. For that length of time, it is basically a self-sufficient spacecraft in itself.

The helmet has built-in cameras, communication devices, and lights. Food and water are placed inside the helmet, within reach of the astronaut's mouth.

The *-oid* suffix in the word *meteoroid* means "like." So a meteoroid is like a meteor. Scientifically, a meteoroid becomes a meteor when it enters Earth's atmosphere.

The bright orange suits worn during launch are designed for emergencies. If the space shuttle **decompresses**, the suits inflate to maintain air pressure on the astronauts' bodies. If the astronauts land in water, the suits keep them warm and have parachutes and life rafts.

The suit inflates to create air pressure on the body.

The space suit has oxygen tanks in a pack on the back. Filters take away the poisonous carbon dioxide breathed out by the astronaut.

Did You Know?

Why would an astronaut's blood boil in the vacuum of space? Think of how a bottle of soda fizzes when you open it. Under normal air pressure, some of the gases we inhale get dissolved in the blood and body tissues. In outer space, there is almost zero air pressure. Without air pressure on the body, these gases would expand and try to escape. When gas molecules escape a liquid such as blood, they make the liquid boil.

The helmet visor is gold-coated. This reduces glare from the sun.

SHOCKER
Astronauts have an embarrassing secret under their space suits – diapers! There is no way of going to the bathroom during a space walk.

The astronaut is kept cool by a system of tiny cooling pipes woven into the fabric of a special undergarment.

Preparing for Space

Preparing astronauts for the conditions in space isn't easy. For a start, in space you are weightless. Astronaut training programs can come close to simulating the experience of spaceflight, but they cannot re-create it exactly. Shuttle astronauts train at the Johnson Space Center in Houston, Texas. Over the years, NASA has devised ways of giving trainee astronauts that "real space feel" here on Earth.

Shuttle astronauts also spend hundreds of hours practicing for different kinds of launch emergencies. If something goes wrong soon after liftoff, the crew and Mission Control have only minutes to decide on a course of action.

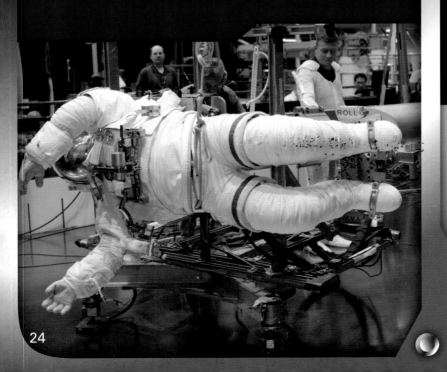

Space Walk Mockup

In the Space Vehicle Mockup Facility in Texas, astronauts practice for space walks. This astronaut is attached to the training version of the robotic arm of a space shuttle.

Training Tricks

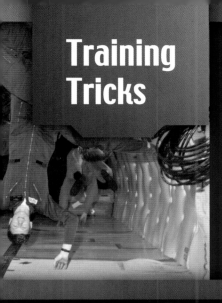

The Vomit Comet

To experience **zero gravity**, trainee astronauts are given a roller-coaster ride in a specially **modified** airplane. At the top of each "hump," the airplane begins to dive and the passengers become weightless for about 25 seconds. At the bottom of each dive, the pilot pulls up sharply and everyone is pressed to the floor by a strong force. On these flights, even people with strong stomachs can feel queasy. It's no wonder astronauts call the airplane the "Vomit Comet"!

Pool Practice

Being under the water isn't the same as being weightless in space. However, it is a helpful practice for adjusting to the effects of Newton's laws of motion. This means that if you push something while floating in space, you will move backward with an identical force. Astronauts prepare for space walks by learning how to use tools and move objects in a huge pool.

Emergency Evacuation

Shuttle astronauts have to train for the possibility of having to evacuate from the shuttle over the ocean. They all take part in emergency and water-survival training sessions.

Space Station

The space shuttle is playing a major role in the biggest project in space – the International Space Station (ISS). The ISS is an orbiting science lab being built by space agencies from around the world. When it is completed, it will contain six laboratories, as well as living, storage, and service areas. Each module is being brought to space separately. Astronauts connect the parts in space.

Eventually, crews of as many as six will live and work on the ISS for six months at a time. The first crew of three arrived on November 2, 2000. Unmanned supply rockets deliver water, food, and fuel. Power comes from wing-like solar panels. Air is produced by extracting oxygen from water. In case of emergency, the ISS has two Russian spacecraft standing by to act as life rafts.

The ISS is designed mainly for scientific study. Experiments will be conducted on the effects of weightlessness on plants and small animals, and the behavior of fluids in space. It is hoped that these experiments will lead to advances in medicine and technology.

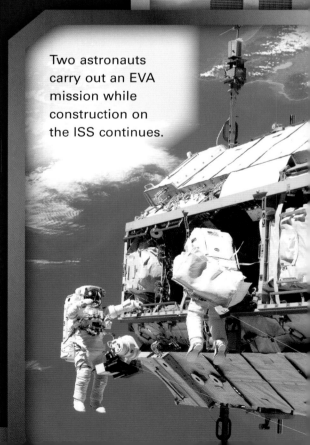

Two astronauts carry out an EVA mission while construction on the ISS continues.

The ISS is made up of several modules built by various different space agencies.

Begun:
November 1998

Planned completion:
2010

Orbit:
about 220 miles above Earth

Time to orbit Earth:
92 minutes

Partner countries:
U.S., Russia, Japan, Canada, Austria, Belgium, Brazil, United Kingdom, Denmark, France, Germany, Italy, Netherlands, Norway, Spain, Sweden

SHOCKER
Dennis Tito's eight-day trip into space cost $20 million!

What Do You Think?

On April 28, 2001, a new era in space travel began. The world's first space tourist, an American businessman named Dennis Tito, visited the ISS. He flew there in a Russian *Soyuz* rocket. People who are wealthy enough can now pay to travel into space. Some people believe that space travel will soon be as affordable as airplane travel. Do you think "space tourism" is a good idea?

Justifying an Opinion
• reread the issue carefully
• try to state both sides of the issue
• review available evidence
• form and state your opinion
• be prepared to support your opinion with evidence

27

Watch This Space

On April 24, 1990, the space shuttle *Discovery* headed skyward with an especially precious cargo – the Hubble Space Telescope. The telescope is named after Edwin Hubble, an American astronomer. Hubble is a bus-sized telescope that orbits Earth. Ordinary telescopes view the stars through Earth's blurry atmosphere. In space, however, starlight is clear and steady. Hubble can see much better than Earth-based telescopes. Hubble collects light with an eight-foot-wide mirror. It sees **visible light** as well as light that our eyes can't see, such as infrared and ultraviolet light.

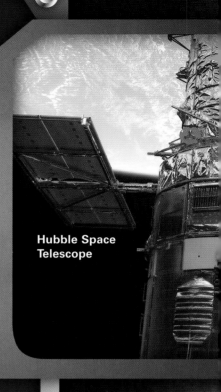

Hubble Space Telescope

Hubble has provided scientists with thousands of astonishing images. The images have taught us about the size, age, and structure of the universe. The most amazing thing about Hubble is that it lets us look back in time. Many galaxies are so distant that their light takes millions of years to reach us. When we view these galaxies through Hubble, we are actually seeing a picture of how the universe looked long, long ago.

Scientists were shocked when early pictures from Hubble looked fuzzy. It turned out there was a flaw in the telescope's main mirror. It took three years of planning and a space walk to solve the problem. Since then, Hubble's cameras have captured amazing images of the universe. Colors are often added to the images to bring out certain features.

I already know something about the Hubble Space Telescope. I remember seeing some spectacular images of other galaxies on the Web. Reading is easier when you already know something about the topic.

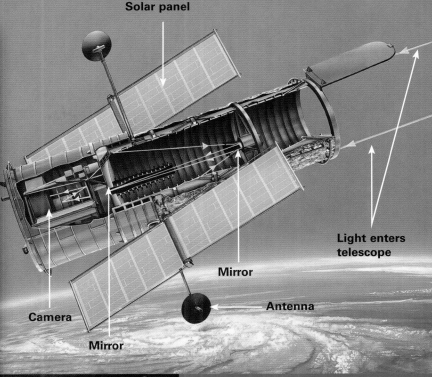

Solar panel

Light enters telescope

Mirror

Antenna

Camera

Mirror

Image of a **supernova** taken by Hubble

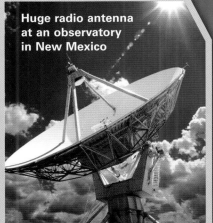

Huge radio antenna at an observatory in New Mexico

What Do You Think?

People have long wondered about life on other planets. Scientists believe that it is unlikely that intelligent life exists elsewhere in our solar system. They have turned their attention farther afield. Using huge radio antennas, they look for unusual radio signals from space. Such signals could be evidence of **extraterrestrial** technology. Do you think money, time, and effort should be spent trying to find extraterrestrial life in space?

29

The Future Is Out There

In 2010, the space shuttles will be retired. However, space exploration will continue. NASA will replace the space shuttles with the new *Orion* crew exploration vehicle. A return to the moon and manned missions to Mars are both planned. Other missions will keep up the search for life on other worlds.

Why do we continue to spend billions of dollars on space missions when there are so many problems to be solved on Earth? One reason is that the unique conditions in space may help us invent new technologies and improved medical techniques. Another reason is that space still holds many mysteries. In space, we may at last find the answers to some of humankind's oldest questions: How was the universe created? How did life begin on Earth? How might it end?

"Made on the Moon"

In 2005, NASA unveiled new plans to return to the moon. Future missions may establish a settlement near the moon's south pole. The settlement would help prepare astronauts for future missions to Mars. Private companies would be invited to set up businesses there.

Space Exploration

Pros
- invent new technologies
- find answers to age-old questions
- unique conditions for research

Cons
- money could be used on Earth
- places on Earth still to be explored

The *Orion* will be similar in shape to the old *Apollo* spacecraft, but will be larger and have the newest technology.

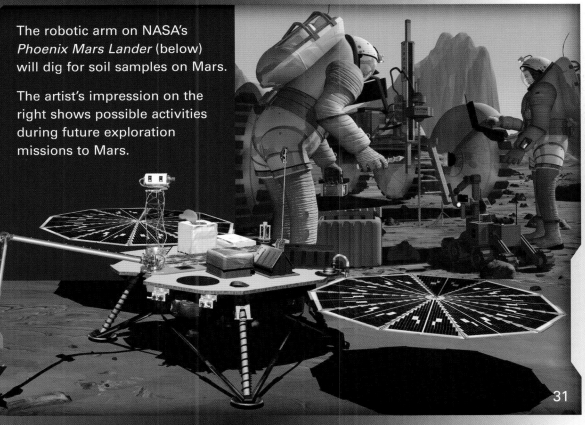

The robotic arm on NASA's *Phoenix Mars Lander* (below) will dig for soil samples on Mars.

The artist's impression on the right shows possible activities during future exploration missions to Mars.

When you look up at the moon, do you see the face of an old woman or the shape of a rabbit, as some do? Or do you see a vacation resort and an untapped source of minerals? This is how some businesses view the moon. Already, several businesses are taking bookings for tourist flights around the moon. Others are looking at ways to build hotels there. Some see the moon as a possible source of raw materials that may be rare on Earth.

WHAT DO YOU THINK?

Do you think we should allow businesses to exploit the moon or other planets?

PRO

I believe business has an important role in the future of space. Space can't be polluted because nothing lives there now. Also, competition between companies will speed up the exploration of space and increase our knowledge of the universe.

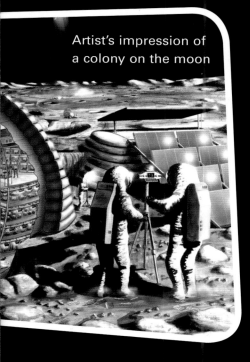

Artist's impression of a colony on the moon

The moon may contain large quantities of a substance called helium 3, which could be sent back to Earth to produce electricity. Some people believe that as Earth's resources are used up, we must look to space for our future needs. However, others believe that businesses are mostly interested in profit. They fear the moon will become polluted or damaged, as are parts of Earth, if we allow the moon to be exploited.

CON

I don't believe businesses should be allowed to exploit space. Companies are not allowed to set up factories or mines in Antarctica, for example. Space is unspoiled. It should stay that way.

GLOSSARY

Cold War a highly tense period of conflict between the U.S. and the USSR in the second half of the twentieth century

combustion (*kuhm BUSS chuhn*) the process of catching fire and burning

commemorative (*kuh MEM uh ruh tiv*) made or done to honor and preserve the memory of an event or a person

decompress to release from pressure

extraterrestrial coming from outer space

friction (*FRIK shuhn*) the force that slows down an object whenever it touches something else, such as a surface

ignite to catch fire or cause to catch fire

jettison (*JET uh suhn*) to throw out something that is no longer needed

lava (*LA vuh*) melted rock that has come out of a volcano

meteoroid a chunk of space rock that is smaller than an asteroid

modify to change something slightly to serve a new purpose

oxidant a substance containing oxygen that reacts chemically with other substances

payload bay a special compartment on the space shuttle that carries satellites

Meteoroid

promote to contribute to the advancement of something

reentry the return of a spacecraft to Earth's atmosphere

satellite any object that orbits a larger object, such as a moon or a spacecraft orbiting a planet

supernova the explosion of a star

thrust the forward force produced by the engine of a jet or rocket

unconscious (*un KON shuhss*) not awake and aware; not able to see, feel, or think

visible light the part of the electromagnetic spectrum that humans can see

FIND OUT MORE

BOOKS

Johnson, Rebecca L. *Satellites*. Lerner Publishing Group, 2005.

McNeese, Tim. *The Space Race*. Children's Press, 2003.

Nipaul, Devi. *The International Space Station: An Orbiting Laboratory*. Children's Press, 2004.

Simon, Seymour. *Destination: Space*. HarperCollins, 2006.

Thimmesh, Catherine. *Team Moon: How 400,000 People Landed Apollo 11 on the Moon*. Houghton Mifflin, 2006.

WEB SITES

Go to the Web sites below to learn more about travels in space.

www.nasa.gov/audience/forkids/home/index.html

www.discovery.com/stories/science/iss/iss.html

www.kidsastronomy.com

www.esa.int/esaKIDSen/LifeinSpace.html

www.bbc.co.uk/science/space/exploration/missiontimeline

INDEX

ABOUT THE AUTHOR

Peter Rees lives and writes in Wales, in the United Kingdom. One of his earliest memories is watching the *Apollo 11* moon landing on TV. The closest he has gotten to space was launching a model rocket on his brother's farm. When Peter saw how quickly the rocket left the ground, he decided that writing about space travel was a lot safer than actually doing it.